MORE 3-D THRILLERS!

BIG CATS

PAUL HARRISON

Capella

What is a Big

T he history of the cat stretches back over 30 million years, and today there are over 30 different species of cat. At the top of this feline pile are the big cats. Although this is a rather loose group, when people talk about big cats they often mean tigers, lions, leopards, cheetahs, cougars, and jaguars.

WHAT BIG TEETH YOU HAVE

30 million years of history have bred some extraordinary cats. One of the most famous was the sabre-tooth cat, sometimes known as the sabre-toothed tiger. This fearsome predator had a massive pair of pointy teeth which it used to stab its prey. It lived in North and South America, but don't worry—it died out about 10 thousand years ago.

SAME DIFFERENCE

All cats are basically the same, whether it's the humble tabby or the majestic lion. They all have an excellent sense of smell and sight, and like to keep clean. All cats are carnivores, too, which means they are meat-eaters—and the bigger the cat, the bigger the meal they need.

Big cats are found in the wild on every continent except Antarctica, Australia, and Europe.

Cat?

UNDER THREAT

Despite being top predators, many species of big cat are under threat of extinction. Some cats are hunted for their skins which are used to make clothes or rugs, or are killed for their bones and teeth, which are used in some traditional medicines. Even though these cats are protected they are still hunted by poachers. Cats are also facing the loss of their habitat as human populations expand. When big cats and humans get too close together problems arise, especially when farmers lose their animals to hungry cats.

NOW YOU SEE THEM

Spotty or stripy, or even a plain dusty brown color, each type of cat's coat serves the same purpose —it helps them to hide. All big cats have to catch their food, so the longer they can stay hidden from their prey the more chance the cat has of sneaking up and catching it.

WHAT'S BEING DONE?

Many organizations are trying to protect big cats. One way is to educate people as to how important big cats are to the local economy. A dead cat can bring big money for poachers, but a live cat can bring in more money from rich tourists who want to see the cats in the wild. Also, farmers don't mind losing cattle so much if they are paid for each animal that gets eaten by a cat.

Tigers

The tiger is the most recognizable of all the big cats, with its orangey-red stripy body. It is also the biggest of all big cats, with the Siberian, or Amur, tiger being the biggest species of all. These huge cats can grow up to 13 feet long and weigh as much as four people.

WHERE ARE THEY FOUND?

Tigers can be found in India, Siberia, and South-East Asia. There are five types of tiger alive today, but there used to be more spread across a much bigger area.

GOOD MOTHER

Tigers are solitary creatures, like most big cats, except when a mother tiger is raising her young. Tiger cubs stay with their mothers for around 2 years until the cubs leave to find their own territories. During those years, the mother will teach her cubs how to survive in the wild. One of the most important lessons is how to stalk and hunt prey —if you don't eat, you don't survive.

MAN HUNTER

Tigers are one of the few big cats who will occasionally hunt people as their prey. This is particularly true in the Sunderban region of Bengal, India. This large area is made up of mangrove trees growing where three rivers meet the sea. People don't actually live there, but do visit to collect wood and hunt. However, tigers kill people there every year. Knowing that tigers like to sneak up on their prey, the wily locals started to wear masks on the back of their heads so a tiger creeping up from behind would think it had been spotted.

FANCY A DIP?

Like pet cats, some big cats hate the water. Not the tiger though, which likes nothing better than a relaxing swim in a cool river or pond.

No two tigers have the same stripy pattern on their coats. Each tiger's coat is unique —a bit like your fingerprints.

Lions

The lion is often called the king of the beasts, and it's easy to see why, with its regal appearance. Although it's true that lions are not the biggest cats in the world, they are certainly kings of all they survey in their own territories.

TEAM WORK

Lions are not the fastest of the big cats, which you would think might be a problem when hunting speedy gazelles or swift zebras. However, they get round this by hunting as a team. Generally, it's the lionesses that do all the hunting, but when it comes to eating it's the males who eat first—that doesn't really seem fair, does it?

SOCIABLE CATS

Lions are social animals, which makes them something of a rarity in the cat world. They are the only cats to live in family groups, which are called prides. The head of the pride is the dominant male lion.

WHERE ARE THEY FOUND?

Lions used to be found in Africa, Asia, and even Europe, but are now restricted to India and Africa. Even here they're not particularly widespread, with the cats found only in certain parts of Africa and one area of India.

SLIM PICKINGS

Even though lions are sociable, it's still a rough life for the cubs. They are always last to feed after a kill and it's not unknown for some cubs to starve to death if there's not enough meat to go round. Worse still, if a new lion becomes the pride's dominant male he is likely to kill the cubs of the old one.

Strangely, lion cubs are born with spots—as the cubs get older, the spots disappear.

MANE ATTRACTION

Male lions are the only members of the cat family to have a mane. Nobody is exactly sure what it's for, but many scientists presume it's for making the lion look good and attracting lionesses. Interestingly, a recent study found that the darker the lion's mane, the more attractive the lion was to females. It seems that in the world of the lion, blondes don't have more fun.

Leopards

T he leopard is one adaptable cat—it can live in all sorts of different environments and will hunt many types of animal, from lizards to baby giraffes. It is also the most widespread of the big cats and comes in a whole range of different sizes, depending on where it lives.

Some leopards' rosettes are a roundish shape and others' are square, depending on where the leopard is from.

WHERE ARE THEY FOUND?

Leopards are found in Africa, India, Siberia, China, and Indonesia. They can live in forests, grasslands, and even mountainous areas, depending on the country.

BLACK PANTHER

Some leopards are born almost completely black in color and are sometimes known as panthers. No one knows why this is, but there seem to be more panthers born in areas with thick jungles. Perhaps a dark coat would be even harder to see here. If you look closely at the coat —though this is not recommended in the wild! —you will see that it still has dark spots and rings, called rosettes.

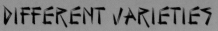

DISAPPEARING TRICK

A leopard's coat is covered in rosettes. This odd patterning is excellent for helping it hide in trees or long grass. In fact, the leopard is one of the stealthiest hunters on the planet and is expert at creeping right up on its prey without the unfortunate animal realizing.

DIFFERENT VARIETIES

There are more than 20 species or subspecies of leopard, and they come in all sorts of shapes and sizes. In fact, some scientists believe that two sorts of leopard, the clouded leopard of the Indonesian islands and the snow leopard of Siberia are different enough from normal leopards to be classed as a different species entirely.

FOLLOW ME

Being so good at hiding does have its downside—it makes it very difficult for your cubs to find you or follow you in the grass. Leopards help overcome this problem the same way tigers do, by having bright white patches behind their ears which the cubs find easy to spot.

TREES

Leopards are great climbers and spend a lot of time up trees either sleeping or hunting. Trees serve another useful purpose—they're a great place for leopards to hide their food. After making a kill, leopards are anxious that some other predator, such as a lion, will steal it—so they carry the bodies into the trees for safe-keeping. This takes great strength, as sometimes a kill can weigh up to three times what the leopard weighs itself.

Cheetahs

T he cheetah is the great specialist of the cat world and has developed into a lightning-fast hunting machine. But life is still pretty hard for cheetahs. Once they could be found throughout Africa, the Middle East, and in India, but now these sleek, speedy animals are an endangered species.

Cheetahs have two large black lines running down their faces from their eyes. These marks make it look like the cheetah is crying.

WHERE ARE THEY FOUND?

It used to be thought that cheetahs could only hunt on the open plains of the African savannah but, in fact, cheetahs are also found in mountainous areas. There are cheetahs in many parts of Africa, and there may even be small population in Iran.

FAST CAT

Cheetahs are not only the fastest of the big cats, they are the fastest land animal on the planet. These speedy cats can reach around 62 miles per hour, which is nearly as fast as cars can legally travel on the freeway. Such a talent for speed comes in handy when chasing lunch across the plains, but the cheetah can't run this fast for very long. Usually it will give up chasing after about 20 seconds, though sometimes a chase will last as long as a minute.

SPEEDY BUT WEEDY

Extreme speed has its downsides, however. The cheetah is quite a light-weight cat, which is great for traveling fast, but bad for fighting. Often a cheetah will catch its prey, only to have it stolen by a bigger, meaner predator such as a lion, hyena, or even a baboon. So, although cheetahs have a high hunting success rate compared to other big cats, they can still go hungry.

ROYAL CONNECTIONS

Cheetahs are one of the easiest cats to tame and were once the fashionable pets of ancient royalty. In fact, it is believed the cheetahs have been caught as pets for over 5,000 years. The cheetahs were used as hunting cats by royalty from Sumeria to Europe, who used the cheetahs' awesome speed to catch other animals.

CHIRPY CHIRPY CHEEP CHEEP

Cheetahs don't roar, like some of the big cats. Instead, they make an odd little noise which sounds like chirping. When annoyed they hiss, and when happy cheetahs make a loud purring noise—just like a big tabby cat.

Cougars

The sleek and athletic cougar is the most widespread of American big cats. In some parts of America it is still legal to hunt these magnificent animals, though many people are trying to stop this.

WHERE ARE THEY FOUND?

Cougars are found from southern Canada right down to Patagonia in South America. However, their distribution is patchy, and many populations are becoming isolated by new housing developments blocking off the links between each area they inhabit.

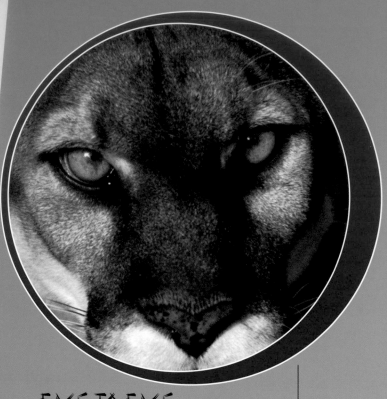

FACE TO FACE

Occasionally, people and cougars come face to face. If it happens to you, the trick is to make yourself look as big as possible and stare the cougar straight in the eye. If you're wearing a jacket, spread it out like a big cape behind you. Never bend down as this makes you look more like cougar food. Never take your eyes off the cougar and don't turn round.

OH SO SECRET

Even though cougars live over such a huge area of both North and South America, very few people have actually seen them in the wild. There are a couple of reasons for this. Firstly, cougars hunt at dawn, dusk, and night so there are fewer people around at those times to see them. And secondly, cougars are very shy animals and will usually go out of their way to avoid people.

BURIED TREASURE

Like many big cats, once a cougar has made a kill it wants to keep hold of it. However, the cougar doesn't hide its food in trees like a leopard—instead it cleverly buries its kill under a pile of leaves and dirt. With its food safely hidden, the cougar returns to it every night until it's all gone.

Cougars are called a variety of names including puma, mountain lion and Florida panther.

PAIN IN THE NECK

Cougars aren't fussy eaters and will eat almost anything from deer and beaver to insects and even snails. Cougars like to sneak up on their prey in the same way other big cats do, and when their food is close by, the cougar pounces on it with one mighty leap. However, unlike other the big cats, a cougar doesn't strangle its prey but breaks its neck with a bite from its powerful jaws.

Jaguars

The greatest South American predator is the jaguar. Like the leopard, the jaguar is a stealthy night hunter, using its excellent night-vision to track prey. Like most big cats, the jaguar lives on its own and is an expert at hiding in the trees or bushes and, like leopards, some jaguars have black fur, too.

WHERE ARE THEY FOUND?

Jaguars are most common in forested areas of South and Central America, but they are also found in south-western parts of North America. Not all jaguars live in forests though—some are found in desert regions and swampy areas, too.

HEADACHE

Unlike most big cats, jaguars do not kill their prey by biting them around the neck and suffocating them. Instead, jaguars use their powerful jaws and sharp teeth to bite their prey in the head and kill them that way.

GONE FISHING

Jaguars eat a wide range of animals from deer to crocodilians. Jaguars have also developed an ingenious method of fishing. The cat waits by the water and splashes the surface every so often with its tail. For some reason, this attracts fish which are promptly scooped out of the water with the jaguar's paws.

SPOT THE DIFFERENCE

Jaguars are often confused with leopards, but they live on different continents and are a heavier and stockier cat. There is also a subtle difference to their spotty coats. Both jaguars and leopards have a spotty, rosette pattern, but it's the inside of the rosettes which give the game away— jaguars have a few smaller spots inside the rosettes, leopards don't.

Tribespeople often called the jaguar "the beast which kills its prey with one bound."

I CAN HEAR YOU

Jaguars are one of the few members of the cat family which can roar. The other big cats which roar are lions, tigers, and the jaguars' close relatives, leopards.

This edition printed in 2006

Copyright © 2005 Arcturus Publishing Limited
26/27 Bickels Yard, 151–153 Bermondsey Street
London SE1 3HA

Author: Paul Harrison
Designer: Ian Thompson
Editor: Rebecca Gerlings

Picture credits:
Nature Picture Library: Title page; page 3, top left; page 4, top right; page
4, bottom left; page 11, top left; page 12, top right; page 12, bottom left.
Oxford Scientific (OSF)/Photolibrary.com: Page 2, bottom left; page 6,
middle; page 9, middle right; page 9, bottom right; page 10, top; page 13,
top right; page 14 and back cover.
Ardea London Ltd: Page 2, top right; page 3, top right; page 5; page 6,
top; pages 6 and 7; page 7, top; page 9, top left.
NHPA Limited: Page 3, bottom right; page 6, bottom; page 8; page 9,
middle left; page 15, bottom right; page 16.
Bruce Coleman: Pages 10 and 11 and back cover; page 15, top left
The Bridgeman Art Library: Page 11, top right
Science Photo Library: Front cover and page 13, bottom right.
3-D images by Pinsharp 3D Graphics

Printed in China

ISBN-13: 978-1-84193-296-5
ISBN-10: 1-84193-296-5